Later Unearthed

Later Unearthed

Paul Magee

PUNCHER & WATTMANN

© Paul Magee 2025

This book is copyright. Apart from any fair dealing for the purposes of study and research, criticism, review or as otherwise permitted under the Copyright Act, no part may be reproduced by any process without written permission. Inquiries should be made to the publisher.

First published in 2025
Published by Puncher & Wattmann
PO Box 279
Waratah NSW 2298

info@puncherandwattmann.com

NATIONAL
LIBRARY
OF AUSTRALIA

A catologue record for this book is available from The National Library of Australia.

ISBN   9781923099302

Cover image by Saskia Haalebos. "Drift (Alphabet for Modernity)."

Printed by Lightning Source International

Contents

Illusory Things	7
This Belly in Words and Figurines	8
Building Composure	9
From the Ocean	10
Later Unearthed	11
The Isolation of Philosophy	14
Registers	15
The Trolley	16
Taking a Call in Darkness	18
Lighter	20
You Might as Well Drink the Sky	21
Consider	22
Helmet, with Company	23
Catastrophe, Travelling South	24
After the Police have Left	28
Runes	29
Hairdressers	30
X-ray at the Border	31
Very Origins	32
Alcoholic Reunion	33
The Signature Notes	34
'Omnia tempus edax depascitur'	35
Epigrammata	36
Ex Symphonia Armoniae Celestium Revelationum	38
Dreaming in Bourke	40
'Ночь, фонарь, аптека'	49
Сад	50
Буря	52
Необычайное Приключение, Бывшее с Владимиром Маяковским Летом на Даче	53
Три Осени	56
Acknowledgements	58

Illusory Things

Illusory things,
egg-beaters, grammatically-correct sentences, fresh roads,
and alcohol restores us to our reasons,
scent the sense that puts one closest to the ground,
memory an animal fighting
a closed cage,
the clarity of crocodile
launching eight feet from the water
from stationary.
Look them in the eye.
Look them in the mind.

This Belly in Words and Figurines

They are six times our brain size,
landed animals, they dived back in

and the buds of hind-legs
stick out from their skeletons, embarrassed.

Two, and up to nine, stomachs
and James Macpherson, twenty-one, went whaling

off Eden, in Two-Fold Bay, and his harpoon so struck
the krill-sodden pescatarian

that it dived up like a bird through the air
to the bottom of the sea and sounded again

beneath Macpherson's boat which blew up
from the impact of the skull.

Then he and another shot in the air to land inside his whale.
Upon opening of the belly

the colleagues of the two lost sailors, trembling,
found a trousered leg, selfless.

Into death to be born.
And in another stomach nearby doubled-up unconscious

 delirious for one long month, but still thirty years till he'd die,
they found Macpherson. Astounded by survival.

To life he is born, caption to an ocean.
In the echo cathedral stomach around his story.

Building Composure

Most of what we remember we don't.
Templates for generic events
we take as real and colour in.
With the feeling of being there
we derive from being here, breathing,
and "I thought" is never verbatim the words that were.
Writing is a world
where oceans are tiny.

*

Write about time someone lied to you violently
but compassionately, write about your liar compassionately.

*

A trade, that's no exchange. To default
is the default. It exacts beyond the life.
God would be the one who looks behind the wall.
We die exactly.
That death mask, that jubilatory welcome.

From the Ocean

Open air, open water, plummeting
through a selflessness so cut-off from others it's beyond all caring,
the sea is one great shock.

Dive between breaths and your eyes disconnected from each other
by a head.
Work keeps us working,
friends keep us friendly
all this while.

Later Unearthed

Good King George the Fifth
shot thirty-nine tigers in the year nineteen hundred and thirteen.
The mobbers would holler and drive their souls to him.
He dedicated one of these to the Royal Albert Museum
so that tourists greet that dead beast in the afterlife.
They suck your brains out of your nose.
Innards removed.

Good King George of the House of Saxe-Coburg und Gotha,
now Windsor by Royal Proclamation
issued in the thirty thousand one hundred and eighty
sixth issue of the *London Gazette*,
in the war-torn years after he bagged that earth-issued tiger,
plus eight rhinoceri, and a bear
its whereabouts unknown.

These more modern tourists
are here in Heaven, Purgatory, Hell, or Limbo,
curatorial judgement the gate.
Holding back all that dirty matter
to some droplets of the life
that sweats through each caption, but no more.
No more, the reader tourist angel uses their divine eyes for a shield.

For George was then at war with his German cousin Wilhelm the
		Second the Kaiser,
who joked that Shakespeare never wrote the *Merry Wives of Saxe-
		Coburg und Gotha*
and was, like him, cousin to King Haakon of Norway, and Queen
		Victoria
of Spain, and to his own wife
Victoria,
of Teck, once betrothed to Albert his brother who died,
who became Mary, his good queen.

And right down to the moustache, he was
uncannily alike
to his cousin Nicky the Second of Russia
(their Danish mothers both daughters of Queen Louise)
so close, in fact, George could easily have passed
for Tsar to the Tsarina
Alexandra, his former Alix of Hesse-Darmstadt cousin.

Prince Andrew of the House of Schleswig-Holstein-Sonderburg-
		Glücksburg,
Prince of Greece
and of Denmark, and his wife Princess Andrew:
both uncannily alike
to their first cousin King George.
Born Alice Battenberg,
she became Mountbatten because of the war, before adopting her
		husband's name.

George, standard royal.
"Saw *Fidelio*, and damned dull it was,"
but this man appointed the first ever
"Philatelist to the King," and once shot dead in six hours
with a "Perhaps, we overdid it"
pheasants to the number of one thousand
at the four thousand acre Buckingham estate of the First Baron
    Burnham.

His doctor killed him at 11.55
in time for announcement in *The Times*
to run in the morning.
Any later death might have broken in some
(Doctor Dawson's diary, later unearthed)
 "less appropriate" evening journals.

The Isolation of Philosophy

The clowns' workshop begins
with a master insisting you make him laugh
to a stopwatch
your five seconds are up
you are instantly abused.
Its dirty work
takes a week.

From Book One, Chapter Eight of Aristotle's *Politics*.
Although Solon says in one of his poems that no bounds of nature
       hold man back from his greed,
money is an instrument
in the art of household management
and the instruments of any art are finite, what's more
natural law is simply not there to break
but what we strive in our arts to generate.

Registers

the dirt settles down
months and months of subsiding
waves of reality subsiding
we have this ancient practice of keeping words alive
the body lies below it

*

Marcus Aurelius meditated in his German tent
we have two ears, a pair of eyes, both hands
and those binary facts mark us out
for the co-operation stoicism advises
between two sides.

*

The country of euphoria,
multiple entry pass, bribing the drunkest guard.
The forehead must be 18 milimetres from the top
of the photo, face a certain width
eyes not blinking, nor mouth smiling.

*

Eye white page.
The forest is wet.
A black lake pools over windows letters
and people drift through the letters
in their foreign familiar countries

The Trolley

Why do we egotistically assume
the people we borrowed some things from and lazily forgot
to return them a number of times
over the years never replaced them?

I stole Ian's removal trolley.
It's not actually a thing we help ourselves to
on those extended occasions, more a mind.
Ian was hospitalised that time, off work and convinced
he was being kept against his own will
till the psychiatrist came and reminded him.

There was a quartet of paintings by Lewis,
Ian's friend,
each a helmet, nothing else.
He drank wine vile as paint and sported a vile tongue.
There was no other thing on Ian's wall
but that singular concentration
of a squad of four paintings at head height.
Help me shift the insanity
crowding us out of yet another home all these
paintings in life.
I've still got
Ian's weight-bearing wheeled device.

Knowing that he'd make light of it.
Put it in the garage at the back and not mind.
Never seen him since, no idea where else to find him.

Because it is a soul,
a house is full of souls,
you've done this before
I thought the other day as I stared at the trolley
I cannot return and can't own.

Taking a Call in Darkness

You were blindfolded in a smart gallery in Manhattan
and their noise-cancelling headphones
were holding your ear drums stiller than the tongues of the deceased.

Stay as long as you like
taking leave of your senses in a room
you have never perceived.

Walk in, they communicated to your skin.
You stepped hands out, into your
flying thoughts of inside a bullet

lying first against the wall's patience
then head on floor, deaf and blind
just a telephone call from the wall

on the floor spinning
I want to say to you before you died
and then again while crying

on the floor of that squander
and then again on the wall of the floor
with fingers that can't stop scraping

flying at conversation
beyond perception
it is what in the telephone

will always feel dead
and unburied the voice
you cannot hear
in the receiver.

Lighter

A doctor near Dusseldorf
places patients near death
on the most sensitive of scales then weighs them dead
an average 21 grammes
lighter. The weight of our souls?
Maybe the corpses keeping us
anchored by blowing away that anchor?
And a decades-old postcard
so little in the image, my life in the words.
Surely the voices should sound further away.

I don't want the characters in a movie to go.
The credits are there to soften the pic.
You can't have two characters
in a movie who agree with each other,
otherwise they are extras, extras are forever.
He reports his discovering the weight of the soul.
Some people are that little bit lighter.

You Might as Well Drink the Sky

The words we have just heard lodge in an inner ear,
and the sounds have passed, long enough to be grasped.
That second or two
is called the phonological loop and also
known as the immediacy of consciousness.
Understanding any longer utterance
is less echoic, more creative, though rhyming can help to stretch
       memory
making the thing even more forgettably obvious.
The start of the sentence is already going unconscious.

Consider

The government of the government took a survey
and licked the booklet of stamps to mail it out,
saying, "Lesbians and Gays,
should we decide we'll let them marry yes
or: You can debate it really loudly."

"Consider," out of *sidera*, the stars
and *con*, together, a gathering in
of the stars at the core
of Vulcanic analysis.
An absorption.

Most of the time we don't in actual truth
think in words.
Though we do learn
by speaking.

So keep good company
said the Buddha
from a watchful
half-lowered eyelid.

Helmet, with Company

The infantry have one metaphor
that switches back and forth enemy love.
Their trauma being that war
is so exciting, love broken
comparatively, back home.
Gendered, psychotic, ambivalent love disturbs me.
I'm just trying to plant front yard trees into the conversation,
not for anyone to hide behind.
The day holds itself over us like a visor.
It's not that I'm alone in this.
Loss of control most of all
harrows us all.

Catastrophe, Travelling South

1 Stampede

       Winton, North West Queensland

The flooding of a muddy plain
settling a silt of iron-rich dirt into each print
gave to us
three thousand three hundred steps,
stress torsion of a therapod swerving to taste
ninety-five million year old prey
that in the midst of panic can be interpreted
maintaining herd behaviour.
This ball of sunshine, just eight hundred k's
away from the coast, a hundred from the paved road
in forty-three degrees and humid, the hat slips from the sweat of
       your head.
Thoughts come slowly.
We're next.

2 Ending

       The Daintree, North East Queensland

The Daintree forest has been crawling over my book,
attracted by the dim light it reflects,
by the texture of tree flesh.
Syzygium monospermum, Daintree Satinash tree
invites beetles to burrow within.
I have finished reading the Proust
here in the Far North his thoughts
cohabitation, or invasion.
When the cassowary stared at us on the track,

its dinosaur pelt
ignored our ninety-five million year late arrival.
The narrator's climactic sentence
still cleaves to my mind,
"I've decided to marry Albertine" (jealously,
you know it'll end badly).
And truly these trees
tell not years in their rings
but events, as many traumas,
and we write these very thick books with trees.

3 The House in Nature

Josephine Falls, North East Queensland

The waters cool us
gliding on the worn boulder a door of glass unbreakable
because liquid.
A postcard image
pooling in the trees and rocks.
Proust waking rings for the valet.
He rings for the valet
eleven times and only once
rings for the valet
actually the man assures him, arriving at last.
The clarity of consciousness Proust reflects is a dream.
Now I'm reading volume four
in the forest and "valet" is no longer a word
for the work we expect from the world as immediate
as consciousness, but "nature"
is still serving us in this dream.

4 Information

Fires down the eastern seaboard of Australia in late 2019 and early 2020 released over 900 million tons of carbon dioxide, simultaneously placing toxic fumes into beach resorts, towns and cities, including the capital, Canberra, which witnessed an Air Quality Index (AQI) reading of 4,650 on a scale in which 66 and under is regarded as a healthy level in which to exercise, 200 too hazardous to be outdoors without a mask. North Queensland was free of fires at the time. Poem 1 was written while Mt Isa (the nearest recording station) had an AQI reading of 38, *Good, Enjoy Normal Activities* and Canberra 189, *Very Poor, Reduce or Reschedule strenuous Outdoor Activities*. Figures for the Cairns-Daintree area during the composition of poems 2 and 3 were 32, *Very Good, Enjoy Normal Activities*, and 53, *Good, Enjoy Normal Activities*.

5 Heading Back Home

Newell Highway

Tell me what has been lost.
The horizon I never doubted.
I want to drive faster
even if all it will get me is knowledge.
My chest feels brittle.

6 Weather System

O'Connor, A.C.T.

The fire invents its own weather system,
smells comforting, that first second,
the second second realise it's all around you,
a whole city took up smoking last week.
All the air turns black in the minutes
before the fire lands, everyone says,
till then it's the smoky brilliance of orange
I saw staring into the fire as a child, magnified.
The unhealing most brutal
demonstration of aging, creating its own system
and spiraling into the forest.

7 Drought

Breathing is utterly and totally random,
when numbered it is final. More than dice
slipped from the tongue.
More word raised from the well.
But the building is driving us without windows or light.
And houses can write.

If there's a building, there's a thinking
and a sleeping to inhabit, a breathing.
Throw these dice out the fingers of my hand.
Throw these dice out the window of my hand.
Throw my luck out the building of this hand

into a void of hope into a void of fear,

a drought of dark, and change.

After the Police Have Left

Grateful, within hateful, closing that screen door gently, made out of glass, and now in peace and agony. The bodies in it are flying, not letting go of their flight.

I was stone they took her out of my hands, holding on still and casting away. The room is a grave. Never stop there. The after hours never stop.

There's no point to anything but touch.
Its bladed edge be the road we walk down
in its reckless flight through the air.
Not knowing you there
where we used to
seconds back.
You cut me beyond trust.

Your kisses plant me in some other mind.
Police have left.
There's no law
in that room and nothing to exchange.
It is not found anywhere else in this globe.

Runes

The rocks are paved in the shapes of waves
in the hall of observing in silence.
And their vases are hollow
and bowls empty
and coins are for conjure.
All the inks in all the books of all the libraries
are dry.

Hairdressers

> 1991

The hairdressers were there at the station and greeted us,
nunchukus in their back pockets in case those blank blank
fascists put the boot in again. Yulia was the girl
I'd met on the train, her boyfriend, a Turkman, stepped forward.

A flame eternal on the burner in the kitchen
at their hostel, gas as common as air
but matches scarce just then, karate poster on the wall,
sockets not earthed: no plugging appliances in.

Also at the blank Hairdressing Academy crashing, Oleg
the friend from Ashgabat, an elevator repairer
who had just left his job a month ago, for a while, it seemed
it would always be there, there's always a set of stairs you don't want
      to climb

and no lift, to repair, and they did all our hair
the time we bussed into town, looked up and down
the old city like tourists for my visitor's sake
and no one attacked us. Thank God.

I don't think I was scared, just stupid in my youth, and amused
by it. Yulia had an East German set of scissors,
the sublime scissors in the Soviet Union of that day, which
was cracking up, but people still nurtured each other's best look,

went out and loved, would still house a weird stranger
in spite of the racist outside, and by the icon of Bruce Lee
slowly swapped nunchukus for scissors. Why I
remember this now? Each new haircut in their name.

X-ray at the Border

Take this little bit of luggage, all I carry.
I only ever hear from grief, have my phone.
But I can tell you just what it's like to be dead.
Turn the page, arms folded.
Recalling a name.
My own.
Is there constant experience of anything?

There is something flesh on bone but less
than named staring through us
as everywhere a border
that is nowhere
the same
line of sight:
writers are witnesses that they
sit still,
in full type

less than named
arms folded
staring through.

I cannot remember but still witness.

Very origins

Beer in plastic cups in the once most bombed hotel in all Europe,
chandeliers set in the ceiling
like so many fragments,
and the men beside me pour out slogans I cannot understand
from their beer, but they look like me.
It's the third row at the wrestling, and kids
are bubbling beside us, referees get punched
knocked-out twice.

I am wrestling with nothing.
Depression has no roots
in a country I go
to spell my name out
and don't need to, they know.

And this grandmother hobbles over
to console some body drooping from the ropes
and your compere gently escorts her home
to her seat, what is she
a plant, a relation, drunk.
She, having flown into a room
of masked men, women in tights and fire boots,
the stage thudding—
she is wrestling with nothing, *I am.*
For what surrounds us has no roots, but everywhere.

Alcoholic reunion

Thirty years on, there's so much to say.
The wine is spilling freely, it's the blood of our compact.
Keep it pumping like a handshake, an aorta,
saying nothing about no one, in response to nothing, bodies age.
Sleep snakes us all away and dreams
we are in the moment.
Recognition is an insanity.
Colour, an accident of words.
I wake sluggish this morning, teeth yellow in the mirror,
history coiled around the moment, tender sides winding
down the hall for a feed on some eggs to swallow whole,
these predators within look out with beady eyes.
Branches all along the path flung up to look like snakes
that leap out of winter packed with venom.
Alcohol and tobacco are our psychiatrists.
It is a fact that they cure you.
Death mutters in everyone's ear.
Obstacles to writing.
That it's a fiction in any genre.
It is a fact that they kill you. They kill fiction.

The Signature Notes

You hear a voice speaking
and rearrange
what it said that you thought,
in writing.
The past speaks over the top of us.

'Omnia tempus edax depascitur'

'Time eats everything up'

Time eats everything up—it snatches it all
from the root. Nothing's for long here.
Rivers lose heart. The beach is desert.
Exiled, the sea. Tallest mountains fall.
Why chatter? The giant sky's beauty
will burn to a cinder again. Suddenly
not as punishment but law everywhere
death insists. And away with worlds.

    Seneca, 41-49

Epigrammata

Epigrams I.32, I.77, I.1, I.88, I.38

I don't like you, Sabidus, and I can't say why
but what's clear is this: I don't like you.

*

Charinus is in splendid health and yet looks pale.
Charinus only sparingly drinks and yet looks pale.
Charinus digests as he should and yet looks pale.
Charinus resolutely suns but still looks pale.
Charinus is dying his skin but still looks pale
and if it's pussy he licks he still looks pale.

*

Look! It's the poet you were waiting for,
Martial, and now you're reading him,
famous over the globe for his vivid books
of epigrams. You've given him, zealous reader,
while alive and able to enjoy it,
glory such as few poets know in the grave.

*

Alcimus, ripped from your master, still growing into a man,
the earth round Labici covers you lightly.
No tumbling pile of heavy Parian marble
for you and your ashes, architectural labours
that one day will fall. Accept from me instead, dear child,
these easily-got bordering shrubs, the thick
shade of some vines and, dewy with night, a grassy lawn

growing brightly, this monument of my grief.
An offering to you, that won't die so young.
When the three Fates have spun my years to an end,
I want my ashes to be laid like yours in a garden.

*

You're reading my poetry, Fidentinus,
but when you read it so badly,
it starts to become yours.

      Martial, 86

Ex Symphonia Armoniae Celestium Revelationum

from 'Symphony on the Harmony of Celestial Revelations'

1 Antiphon for the Creator

The miraculous
knowledge in God's heart
of all Creation

was older
for when God looked into the face of man
he saw, whole there,

every one of his works
thus
waking us.

2 Antiphon for God the Father

Please Father,
it would be right.
Look on us

with your Name, that we not break
and fall through, that it not
be obscure within us

for
through your very Name,
you release.

3 Responsory for Saint Disbod

Joying soul, your body was born of the Earth
and you stepped on that body
again and again in your wandering the world.

That is why you were crowned in God's thought,
it made you its mirror,
Divine Spirit saw you for a home.

You were crowned in God's thought.
Which made you its mirror.
It is why.

4 Antiphon for Saint Ursula

Ruby of blood flowing
from the highest skies
next to God.

You are the flower winter
has never lesioned with
its serpent's breath.

       Hildegaard of Bingen, 1151

Dreaming in Bourke

Town

A seat outside the police station in the silence
on the Sabbath of no God. Forty-five degrees
all cars to the curb, parked
and empty. The only police in this place
ghosts. Only ghosts.
Here the shouting of iced-up teens on bikes.

Gone too now, the good folk
from the night before in the Bowls Club, where the chow mein
was crisper than the freshest memories and we laughed.

Patted the dog like a coffin barking
with words out its mouth
the night of the day we arrived in Bourke
where the streets are grid on disorderly desert
cars at forty-five degrees and not a soul to promenade.
That little coffin stirring, yawning, barking mad
with iced-up teens in hoods scaring the paving
to emptiness. There's no one in the street

grid in red dirt
neat as the pattern
cages hold out to the world
and let the world through:

They die young here, Paul said.

Own

Landscape written large above us
in this little town below.
Court House, locked up and dark.

Other houses are thinking repairs
behind the boards that stand for
windows here.
Streets wider than rivers
path through the sky. So I leave

the hotel compound
for a walk, down the disturbing street,
stopping to write in the floral bower
opposite a Cop Shop
we sell time
ricochet back from the shouting.

On the threshold of the compound
Paul meets me, Wayne a little further inside, both meet me,
they were going to come get me from my crazy
walk into the Sabbath in Bourke
where ganged youth get high
might cherish a knife
at me for money, which flows

into drugs,

which flows into the soothing

keeping us all safe, and looked-after.

Barkindji live here, have no land, the one claim
given back as National Park,
yesterday we drove out there, Road Closed
to Wayne and Paul who own it.
The whites exclude them like ghosts
and are haunted. Here in the motel
Wayne, not staying, was told off
by the motel owner for parking
inside the compound
on the land he and Paul own. Pizza
under the stars there later in the night.

Barkindji: still owned by the stars
which are land and river and animal too
keeping us safe, and looked-after.
"I was gonna come after you soon, Bud.

You don't go out there on your own."

Old Shed

And a guy on the nearby banks of the Barka
showed us a painted emu egg
he was selling, unwrapped it from
the tea towel and its colours
intense and local as the dot of the Earth,
to see it advertised was to hold it
in the soft red dirt of your mind.
To hold it still, hatched
as the emus that flocked yesterday's dirt road.
It's Country, gazetted or not.
The radio in our ears at Toorale

sending out birds more numerous than the thoughts
you can see clearly
at each landing in the mind. A headfull of birds
in each call trail through the mind, already there
and another arrives, the words of the Warego flowing by us
and through at the old shed, where we recorded ghosts
that don't even need to advertise
they're beyond exchange, being.

The Fountain

Tall shelves over each aisle,
in rivers of stuff for the deep fryer,
and at the cashier
young kids who grew up here at home
in the Sun, and the light,
and the fluorescent
green from the trees, and the river
overflows under the bridge, and may be
cut off on Thursday
when flood is predicted again
by the telly in the Bowls Club,
opposite, the Court House.
Its darkened brows,
wait for the next day of judgement.

I'm sure to shave every morning out here.
You don't want your face to grow landscape.

It'll settle down roots in the river,
tree in flood, it won't want to leave.

You'll grow friends, you'll be chatting
for ages with Brian in the gallery,

Paul's cousin, a cousin of cousins,
who gave you a turtle painting

even though you paid him for it,
it's wrapped in bubble wrap on the shelf

here waiting to float home
to the wall where it'll swim, little turtle

we'll house you there
with the others who river our walls

in our clean-shaven home
hanging on to the soil and writing.

Home, with this fountain pen,
I'm writing home this photograph.

Don't Touch the Egg with your Hands when you Take it from the Nest

The mirror of sunrise
faces the day with sky.
Birds reflect each other in their calls.
And the dragonfly yesterday
women's dreaming
could not be told to me, her shield
of colours a sunrise, in the sunset,
water slowly rising up trees
that have all they can drink inside,
the shore shifts higher.
We'll be in flood
come Thursday with the rain,
it's handed on in pieces.
The future is the past
knowledge you pass on,
be open to
the other side of you as it floods
through the mirror
in a dragonfly you cannot know.
Its colours in the water coming closer,
the floating trees
and sky advancing

Generation

Crease lines run into this rock. Paul asked Kazuki
to try to lift it off the ground.
There's a plaque

declaring the statue of a bale of
wool made of stone, to which it's affixed,
the gift of the pastoralist bestowing upon Bourke this
industry.

At the Port of Bourke wharf the woolly
sculpture sits
waiting for someone to pick it up
to ship, or be read
like the past, that's
everywhere in bits,
too heavy to lift. A park bench sits facing it.

That seat with R U OK
stencilled into it is Bourke's
wait and sit
mental health provider.
It is moving slower than time.

River People

What is it to hear
pain out?

The mist on this sudden lake
is the mist in the distance
on yesterday's pounding rain
within and around us.

There's more than one hospital.
The roads back to Canberra are in flood.

The healing tree Gertie stopped us under.

Paul said, "It's the last time
I'll ever see this country in flood."

'Ночь, фонарь, аптека'

'Night, a street-lamp and a chemist's'

Night, a street-lamp and a chemist's.
This lustreless, meaningless globe.
Take twenty more years, or some more.
No one's ever known an exit.

You'll die. Start it all over again:
everything repeats the past. Night,
an ice-cold ripple in the canal,
a street-lamp and a chemist's.

    Aleksandr Blok, 1912

Сад

Garden

To cope with this underworld
you've sent me, and madness,
make it a garden
for the years that age.

For the years that age,
for the griefs I've to live through,
the years of work coming
and the groanings in my back.

For the years that age.
Bone for that dog.
For the hell-burnt years.
A garden in the breeze

for their refugee.
Bless me with a garden
and nobody there,
a soulless place.

Garden no one steps in.
Garden no one looks in.
A laughterless garden,
a no whistling there
garden.

Earless,
bless me with a garden.
Nothing has a scent there,
not a soul.

Speak: you've tortured enough.
A garden on its own.
But don't come near me here or there.
Yes, he says, it's as alone as me.

That's your garden for me and the years
I age. That. Or your paradise?
Bless me in the years that age.
Deliver me from here.

       Marina Tsvetaeva, 1934

Буря

Storming

> You, poor, naked unfortunates.
> *King Lear, Act III, scene iv*

What's gone mad out the window
the wind hurling the rain
out, like a creature
that howls till dying.

That vile night, it slams into you now,
aches you for the homeless,
is chasing you out
to touch them cold frozen

all in rain and darkness,
common with what they now have.
What's gone mad out the window.
The wind is dying and blasting far away.

    Aleksandr Blok, 1899

Необычайное Приключение, Бывшее с Владимиром Маяковским Летом на Даче

the extraordinary thing that happened to vladimir mayakovsky one summer in a dacha

pushkino akula hill it was the rumantsyevs dacha twenty seven versts from moscow on the yaroslavl line

sunset burned its way through a hundred and forty suns
summer rolled into july
hot it was so hot the heat throbbed
it happened in a dacha
the akula hill is large enough to dwarf
pushkino a mere mound
and at the foot of that mounds a village
pulling faces from its crooked rooves
and beyond that is the hole
into which
the sun daily gets shot
then never fast but surely
having flooded the world
that next morning there rose another scarlet sun
its horribleness scalding me
day in day out i got so pissed off
everything bled with fear
i yelled in its mug
get down from there
stop lolling in the sauna
leech
i yelled youre pampered in clouds while i
can forget about it
winter summer

im endlessly stuck here painting poster after propaganda poster
then yelled again wait listen goldenhead
rather than bludge
come here and have a cuppa
with me what have i done im a goner
toward me of his own free will strode the sun
each step beams of light
i dont want to show im terrified
but then stand back
his eyes already in the garden
now stepping through it the windows doors
and all the cracks in rolled the sun
slumped till hed drawn some breaths
but then began to say in deep bass
im holding back these flames the first time since creation
you called then bring me a cup of tea
bring it with jam
tears in these eyes and heat rising
till im out of my mind gesturing at the samovar
well alright then take a seat o great
lord light bulb
the devil forced my impudence to yell
that at him
he me confused
i sat on the bench edge
afraid this gets much worse
but from him a strange radiance streamed
and formalities all aside
i sat chatting with his luminary of this and of that
and how shat off i am painting propaganda
posters for rosta
he came back i get it okay
stop whining look at it
more simply you think
it easy for me to shine

give it at a go no well its like this you walk
because the idea takes you to take a walk
at the same time you walk
you shine
we chatted like that till dusk
or i mean till former dark
there what darkness was there
began addressing each other informally now as chums
and totally open in our friendship i
slapped him on the back and he replied
you me
the pair of us comrade
get up lets rise
and proclaim to this grey dump of dirt
I will flood it with sun
you with poems
coffin-like walls and prison-like night
both fell at that double-barrel gun
thats me and the sun
a crowd of poems and light
shine as much as you like
and only foolish drowsy sleep
will want night to stretch out suddenly
i will shine fully and day once again
will ring out to shine
at all times to shine everywhere
to the depths of the very last days
and to hell with all the rest
is my slogan for thats the suns

        vladimir mayakovksy, 1920

Три Осени

Three Autumns

The smiles of Summer elude me,
secrets in Winter disappear
but I can catch almost precisely
three Autumns each year.

The first one is all over the place
and it was Summer last night
it's like a day off. Notebook scraps
of leaves blowing, smoky light

incense-sweet and all is soaked
colours and drips, and bright.
The birches, as if leading a dance
in transparent dresses, tremble

in their rush, sprinkling tears
on a neighbour's yard, they won't last.
Their story has only begun,
already, a minute's passed

since the second Autumn's arriving
impassive as clear conscience,
grim as an aerial assault.
Things take on their sudden pallor

feel older, the cosiness of summer is lost,
and the distant marchers in their golden trumpets
float through the fumes of the swirling fog.
The high skies too all in cloud,

behind those cold swirls of incense glint
with death, with howlings and winds
the skies burst through and I know
the illusion coming to an end

is not the third Autumn it is the illusion of breath.

    Anna Akhmatova, 1943

Acknowledgements

Works in this book have previously been published in *Australian Poetry Anthology, Axon, The Canberra Times, Island, Literary Imagination, Mascara Literary Review* and *Meanjin*.

Thank you to John Leonard for helping the words find their way.

www.ingramcontent.com/pod-product-compliance
Lightning Source LLC
Chambersburg PA
CBHW032136090426
42743CB00007B/615